The Wayland Book of
Common British
Wild Flowers

A Photographic Guide

Theresa Greenaway

HODDER
Wayland

An imprint of Hodder Children's Books

The Wayland Book of
Common British Wild Flowers
A Photographic Guide

Cover photograph: A wildflower meadow
Title page: Marsh marigolds growing in a pond.
This page (from top): Germander speedwell; bird's foot trefoil, meadow cranesbill; great burdock.
Contents page (from top): chickweed; common ragwort; field forget-me-not; red clover.

Text copyright © 2002 Hodder Wayland
Volume copyright © 2002 Hodder Wayland

Editor: Polly Goodman   **Designer:** Mark Whitchurch

Photo credits
Eric Crichton 5 (middle & bottom)), 7 (top), 8 (bottom), 10 (all), 11 (bottom), 14 (bottom), 15 (all), 16 (middle), 17 (top), 18 (bottom), 19 (top), 20 (top), 21 (all), 22 (all), 23 (middle), 24 (middle & bottom), 25 (top), 26 (bottom), 27 (bottom), 28 (bottom), 29 (bottom), 31 (top), 33 (top & middle), 34 (all), 35 (all), 36 (bottom), 37 (bottom), 38 (top), 39 (all), 41 (top), 43 (inset), 45; **Ecoscene** Cover (Frank Blackburn) 40 (top), 43 (main); **Hodder Wayland Picture Library** 5 (top), 6 (top), 7 (bottom), 23 (top); **Rowan McOnegal** 14 (top), 29 (top & middle); **Archie Miles** *Title page*, 4 (all), 6 (bulbous buttercups, middle, bottom), 8 (top), 9 (all), 11 (top), 12 (all), 13 (all), 14 (bottom right), 16 (top, bottom left & right), 17 (top), 18 (top), 19 (middle & bottom), 20 (middle & bottom), 23 (bottom), 25 (bottom), 26 (top & middle), 27 (top & middle), 28 (top), 30 (top & middle), 31 (bottom), 32 (all), 33 (bottom), 36 (bluebells), 37 (top), 38 (bottom), 40 (bottom), 41 (bottom), 42, 44; **Papilio** 38 (bottom).

Archie Miles gratefully acknowledges the assistance of Cariann Clarke (flower diary), Freya Guest (seed planting) and the staff at Burley Gate C.E. Primary School.

First published in Great Britain in 2002 by Hodder Wayland, an imprint of Hodder Children's Books.
This paperback edition published in 2003

The right of Theresa Greenaway to be identified as the author of this work has been asserted by her in accordance with the Copyright, Designs and Patents Act, 1988.

British Library Cataloguing in Publication Data
Greenaway, Theresa
    The Hodder Wayland Book of Common British Wild Flowers
    1. Wild flowers - Great Britain - Juvenile literature
    2. Wild flowers - Great Britain - Identification -
Juvenile literature
    I. Title II. Common British wild flowers
    582.1'3'0941

ISBN 0 7502 3896 8

Printed in Hong Kong

Hodder Children's Books
A division of Hodder Headline Limited
338 Euston Road, London NW1 3BH

Contents

What are Wild Flowers?

Wild flowers are flowering plants that grow naturally in the countryside. There are thousands of different kinds, or species, and they are important in many ways. Apart from making our surroundings attractive, wild flowers are part of our heritage and our folklore. Legends about wild flowers that started hundreds of years ago have been passed down from generation to generation, and wild flowers have been used to make herbal medicines since ancient times. Wild flowers are important to animals, too. They provide food for many different insects which, in turn, are eaten by other animals. Deer, voles, mice and rabbits, as well as farm animals, also eat wild flowers.

PARTS OF A WILD FLOWER

A wild flower plant is made up of roots, leaves, one or more stems, and flowers that produce many seeds. Roots anchor the plant into the soil. They also draw up water and dissolved nutrients from the soil, which are essential for the plant's growth. Some types of roots also store food for the plant. The flower is made up of a number of parts, called sepals, petals, stamens and carpels. The sepals cover and protect the inner parts of the flower until it is ready to open The petals attract insects with their colour and scent, and droplets of sweet, sugary nectar produced by the nectaries.

FOOD

The stems and leaves make a wild flower's food. They use the energy from sunlight to combine carbon dioxide from the air with water from the soil to produce simple sugars. This is called photosynthesis. Every plant uses these sugars, as well as nutrients and water from the soil, and oxygen from the air to make all the different chemicals it needs to live and grow.

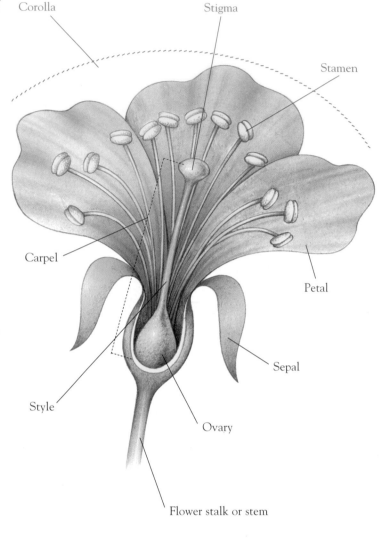

PARTS OF A FLOWER

Corolla

Stigma

Stamen

Carpel

Petal

Style

Sepal

Ovary

Flower stalk or stem

▼ *Perforate St John's wort is used to make a herbal medicine.*

▼ *Orchids are famous for their beautiful flowers, which have a large, central 'lip'.*

▼ *Insects feed on sweet nectar from wild flowers.*

MAKING SEEDS

Wild flowers begin life as seeds. The seeds are produced in the flower, but before a seed can start growing, pollen from the male parts of a flower, called the stamens, has to travel to the female parts, called carpels. The pollen is carried on the bodies of insects when they visit the flowers for food. Attracted by the petals, insects such as bees land on the flower and suck its nectar. Pollen sticks to the bee's hairy body, and when the bee crawls over a different flower of the same kind, the pollen clings to a sticky tip, called a stigma. This is called pollination.

The pollen grains send tiny tubes down into the carpel. The tubes carry the male sex cells, which eventually fuse with the female sex cells. This is called fertilization. Only fertilized flowers can produce new seeds. The seeds grow inside the carpel, which becomes the fruit of the plant. The fruit protects the growing seeds and feeds them all the nutrients they need until they are ready to be released.

HOW SEEDS ARE SPREAD

Wild flowers have to make sure their seeds are spread over a wide area, so the young flowers do not die from overcrowding. Some seeds, such as orchid seeds, are so small and light that they just blow away in the breeze. Others have parachutes of hairs that carry them through the air. Seeds of the pea family are flicked out when the two halves of the pod twist apart. Others, such as agrimony, have fruits or seeds with tiny hooks, which cling to the fur or feathers of animals and birds, and are carried away by them.

FLOWER FAMILIES
Scientists have put wild flowers with similar features into groups called families, for example the pea family and the rose family. You can find out the family of each wild flower in this book by looking at the key facts underneath each heading.

▶ *This butterfly will help pollinate the buttercup it is feeding from by carrying away pollen stuck to its body.*

▼ *Blackberry seeds are dispersed by the animals that eat them.*

▼ *Each dandelion fruit has a parachute of hairs, which helps carry it away in the wind.*

▼ *Great burdock seed heads are covered in tiny hooks, which attach themselves to the fur of passing animals.*

5

Meadow buttercup

Scientific name: *Ranunculus acris*
Height: 30–100 cm
Family: buttercup
Flowering months: April–September

Buttercups are one of Britain's most common wild flowers. Their name comes from the colour of their cup-shaped petals. The meadow buttercup grows along roadsides, along hedgerows, in meadows and in gardens. Like all buttercups it has no scent. Instead, it uses the colour of its bright yellow flowers to attract insects. The sepals are cupped around the shiny yellow petals. The leaves are rounded, and both the leaves and stems are hairy. Bulbous buttercup is very similar to meadow buttercup, but the sepals are bent back from the petals.

▲ *A butterfly lands on a buttercup to drink its nectar.*

◀ *You can tell these are bulbous buttercups because the sepals are bent back and down.*

Creeping buttercup

Scientific name: *Ranunculus repens*
Height: 10–60 cm
Family: buttercup
Flowering months: May–August

▶ *These creeping buttercups are growing in the cracks of a brick floor.*

This plant got its name from the way it spreads itself by thick stems, called runners. The runners grow out sideways from the base of each plant. At the tip of each runner, roots and leaves grow into a new buttercup plant. The new plant sends out its own runners and soon covers an area with buttercups. The lower leaves are divided into three lobes. Each of the three lobes is divided into smaller lobes, with toothed edges. Like the meadow buttercup, the leaves and stems are hairy.

Marsh marigold

Scientific name: *Caltha palustris*
Height: 20–60 cm
Family: buttercup
Flowering months: March–July

Marsh marigold is a sturdy plant with heart-shaped, glossy, dark green leaves with toothed edges. Like buttercups, marsh marigold has flowers with shiny yellow petals. It starts to flower in spring, often as early as March. As its name suggests, marsh marigold grows in damp places such as marshes, ditches, and beside ponds and streams.

▲ *Marsh marigolds growing partly under water in a pond.*

Lesser celandine

Scientific name: *Ranunculus ficaria*
Height: 5–25 cm
Family: buttercup
Flowering months: February–May

The lesser celandine is one of the first signs of spring. Its yellow flowers, each with 7–12 petals and three sepals, start to open in February. Each flower grows singly on a stem. The leaves are heart-shaped with smooth edges, and are often blotched with an irregular, darker green mark in the centre. Lesser celandine grows low on the ground in damp soil, on sunny banks, and in woodlands and hedgerows.

Lesser celandine's flowers are bright yellow and low-growing.

Common poppy

Scientific name: *Papaver rhoeas*
Height: 20–80 cm
Family: poppy
Flowering months: June–August

The common, or field poppy has a branched stem and leaves divided into narrow, toothed lobes. The stems and leaves are usually covered with stiff hairs. Each flower bud is enclosed in bristly sepals, which fall off as the four thin scarlet petals unfurl. These petals often have a purple-black blotch at their base. Many seeds grow in a seed capsule. They can be shaken out through tiny holes which open when the capsule is ripe and dry.

Common poppy is a weed that likes growing on earth that has been broken up or disturbed in some way. This is why it is often seen in fields where grain crops are grown, or on open wasteland.

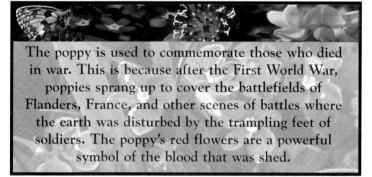

The poppy is used to commemorate those who died in war. This is because after the First World War, poppies sprang up to cover the battlefields of Flanders, France, and other scenes of battles where the earth was disturbed by the trampling feet of soldiers. The poppy's red flowers are a powerful symbol of the blood that was shed.

▶ *Poppies on the edge of a wheat field.*

Shepherd's purse

Scientific name: *Capsella bursa-pastoris*
Height: 3–40 cm
Family: cress
Flowering months: all year round

The shepherd's purse belongs to the cress family. It was named after the shape of its heart-shaped fruits. This family contains many plants that we eat as vegetables, such as cabbages and watercress, but also many that farmers and gardeners regard as weeds. Shepherd's purse is a garden and farmland weed. It can grow in bare soil and even in cracks between paving stones.

At the base of each plant a ring of leaves is arranged like a rosette. Flower stalks grow up from these leaves, with smaller leaves and a cluster of small white flowers, each with four tiny petals. When the petals fall off, heart-shaped fruits grow with seeds inside. Each fruit is on a stalk, which lengthens as the fruit ripens.

◄ *Heart-shaped fruits growing up the stem of a shepherd's purse plant, with a cluster of flowers at the top.*

Garlic mustard

Scientific name: *Alliaria petiolata*
Height: 20–120 cm
Family: cress
Flowering months: April–June

Garlic mustard is usually a tall, stiff plant. The leaves are roughly heart-shaped, with a wavy or toothed edge. When the leaves are crushed they smell strongly of garlic. They are eaten by the caterpillar of the orange-tip butterfly.

At the top of the stem, there are a number of smaller stalks, each bearing many flowers with white petals. Each flower grows into a long narrow fruit on a short stem. When ripe, the sides of this fruit split and curve up, releasing two rows of black seeds.

► *Another name for garlic mustard is Jack-by-the-hedge, because it is a common wild flower of hedgerows and roadsides.*

Cuckoo flower

Scientific name: *Cardamine pratensis*
Height: 15–60 cm
Family: cress
Flowering months: April–June

Like all members of the cress family, cuckoo flower, which is also called lady's smock, has flowers with four petals. The petals are usually lilac-coloured, although they may be very pale and sometimes white. The rosette of leaves at the base of the plant and those growing up the stem are divided into leaflets. The leaflets at the base of the stem are round-shaped, but the leaflets on the stem are long and narrow. Cuckoo flower grows in wet meadows, on the edges of streams and damp roadsides.

The cuckoo flower was given its name because it starts to flower when cuckoos arrive in Britain in the spring. Cuckoos migrate to Britain every spring from their warm winter home in southern Africa.

◀ *Lilac cuckoo flowers are a common sight in spring on damp grassland.*

Red campion

Scientific name: *Silene dioica*
Height: 30–90 cm
Family: pink
Flowering months: May–June

Red campion leaves and stems are covered with soft hairs. The upper surface of the leaves feels slightly sticky. Sprays of flowers open at the top of the tallest stems. Each flower has five pinkish-red petals. The fruit is an oval capsule with tiny teeth at the tip, which open to release the seeds.

White campion and bladder campion are similar to the red campion but, instead of pinkish-red petals, they both have white petals. The sepals of the bladder campion are joined together to make a papery 'bladder'.

◀ *Each of these red campion flowers is about 18–25 mm wide.*

Ragged robin

Scientific name: *Lychnis flos-cuculi*
Height: 30–75 cm
Family: pink
Flowering months: May–June

▶ *The ragged, uneven shape of its flowers gave ragged robin its name.*

Ragged robin is a similar plant to red and white campions, but it has narrower leaves and deep pink petals, each with four, very narrow lobes. Ragged robin grows in damp meadows and marshes.

Chickweed

Scientific name: *Stellaria media*
Height: 5–40 cm
Family: pink
Flowering months: all year round

Chickweed is a spreading plant with branched stems. It is a very common weed of gardens, farmland and wasteland. It has oval, bright green leaves and sprays of small white flowers. The flowers have five petals, each of which has a deep notch at the tip. The green sepals are as long or longer than the petals, and are arranged like a star between each of the petals. Chickweed has a number of similar relatives, including the greater stitchwort, the lesser stitchwort and the bog stitchwort.

▲ *Chickweed plants grow in open clumps of soft, bright-green leaves and white flowers.*

Common dog violet

Scientific name: *Viola riviniana*
Height: 2–20cm
Family: violet
Flowering months: April–June

Common dog violet is one of the most common kinds of violet, but there are many others, including the sweet violet, marsh violet and wild pansy. Common dog violet grows in grassy places, open woodland, hedge banks and pastures. It has heart-shaped leaves. Each flower has five mauve petals, which grow singly on long stems. The lower petal grows backwards from the base of the corolla in a slender, hollow shape, which you can see if you look at the flower from the side. The seeds grow in a capsule with three sections.

◀ *Dog violet relies on colour to attract insects since it has no scent.*

Wood sorrel

Scientific name: *Oxalis acetosella*
Height: 5–15 cm
Family: wood sorrel
Flowering months: April–June

Wood sorrel is a creeping plant, which spreads using underground stems. It sometimes grows in large patches on dry woodland floors, among banks of hedges or shady rocks. Both the leaves and flowers of wood sorrel grow singly at the tip of slender stems. Each leaf is divided into three heart-shaped leaflets. These are attached to the stem by the tip of the 'heart' and hang downwards. The white flowers, each with five petals, are streaked with mauve veins.

▲ *A patch of wood sorrel on a woodland floor.*

Perforate St John's wort

Scientific name: *Hypericum perforatum*
Height: 30–90 cm
Family: St John's wort
Flowering months: June–September

▶ *This plant was hung in houses in Britain and France to ward off evil spirits and ill-health.*

Perforate St John's wort is a stiff upright plant with branched stems. The leaves are oval, and arranged opposite each other. If you hold them up to the light, or look at them through a magnifying glass, you will see that the leaves are covered with almost transparent dots. Other related species, such as the square-stemmed St John's wort, also have these dots on their leaves.

Perforate St John's wort is most common on chalky soils in grassy areas, open woodland or in banks of hedges. Its relative, slender St John's wort, grows in similar places but it prefers chalk-free soils. Slender St John's wort has red-tinged stems and petals, and each petal is fringed with a row of tiny black dots.

Perforate St John's wort has been used as a herbal medicine in Britain and Europe for many years. Recent research has proved that it does help conditions such as depression, but it also reacts unfavourably with some drugs used to treat heart conditions and other complaints, so it has to be used with care.

Common mallow

Scientific name: *Malva sylvestris*
Height: 45–90 cm
Family: mallow
Flowering months: June–September

The common mallow is a large sturdy plant with tough, branching stems. The leaves are almost round, with 5–7 lobes and rounded, toothed edges. Clusters of large pink flowers grow between the leaves and the stems. Bees love the nectar produced by these flowers. The flowers grow into a fruit, which is a ring of nutlets, each containing one seed.

Common mallow is usually found in rough grassy places, on roadsides and beside railways. It can be a pest to gardeners.

Marsh mallows are relatives of the common mallow, with soft hairs. They grow in damp ditches and places near the seaside. The roots of this plant were once used to make the sweets that are still called 'marshmallows', although the plant is no longer an ingredient.

▲ *Mallow flowers have many stamens, which are joined together in a tube-shaped structure.*

11

Meadow cranesbill

Scientific name: *Geranium pratense*
Height: 30–80 cm
Family: geranium
Flowering months: June–September

▶ *You can see the drooping, 'beaked' fruits among the flowers of these meadow cranesbill plants.*

The meadow cranesbill is a widespread wild flower that grows into a clump of leafy, branched stems in meadows and roadsides. Its fruit has a part that sticks out like a beak, or bill, which is how this plant got its name. The lower leaves are divided into lobes arranged like the fingers of a hand. Each lobe is divided into deep narrow teeth. The flowers have five violet-coloured petals.

Herb robert

Scientific name: *Geranium robertianum*
Height: 10–50 cm
Family: geranium
Flowering months: May–September

Herb robert is a red-tinged plant with weak stems, which often sprawls over other plants or rocks for support. The leaves are divided into leaflets, which are in turn divided into many smaller lobes. This gives the leaves a lacy appearance. The small flowers have five petals and are usually arranged in pairs at the tips of stalks. Like the meadow cranesbill, herb robert also has beaked fruits, which snap open in dry weather to flick out the seeds. It grows in woods, gardens, among rocks and on shingly beaches.

◀ *Herb robert can grow almost anywhere – even in this felled beech tree.*

Common bird's foot trefoil

Scientific name: *Lotus corniculatus*
Height: 10–40 cm
Family: pea
Flowering months: June–September

▶ *Common bird's foot trefoil has clusters of small, rounded yellow flowers tinged with red.*

Common bird's foot trefoil has stems that lie almost flat along the ground, or scramble over other low-growing plants. Its leaves are divided into five leaflets. The pea-like flowers are arranged in clusters of between two and seven at the tops of upright stems. Each flower grows into a 3-centimetre-long seed pod, which splits open when ripe. Common bird's foot trefoil can be found in fields, heathlands and other grassy places.

Common bird's foot trefoil was named after its seed pods, which grow stiffly outwards from the stem like the toes of a bird. 'Trefoil' means 'three-leaved'. Another name for this flower is babies' slippers, because of the small, rounded petals.

White clover

Scientific name: *Trifolium repens*
Height: up to 30 cm
Family: pea
Flowering months: June–September

White clover is a creeping plant with trailing stems up to 30 centimetres long. Its leaves and flower stems are upright. Each leaf is divided into three leaflets with finely toothed edges, and each leaflet has a V-shaped mark in the centre of the leaf. Bees are so fond of clover flowers that in rural England, this plant was known as 'bee bread'.

Red clover is similar to white clover, but it has heads of deep pink or reddish-purple flowers and a pair of leaves immediately below each flower head. Both white and red clover are common in fields, banks of hedges and other grassy places. White clover is also a very common weed of garden lawns.

► *White clover has clusters of tightly packed, white or pinkish flowers.*

► *This marbled white butterfly is drinking nectar from red clover using its long straw-like tongue.*

Tufted vetch

Scientific name: *Vicia cracca*
Height: 60–200 cm
Family: pea
Flowering months: June–August

Vetches are climbing plants with long stems. The stems are too weak to support their own weight, so the plants cling to sturdier plants using tendrils. The tendrils coil tightly around the stems of other plants, letting the vetch scramble upwards.

There are a number of species of vetch, and almost all of them have tendrils. Tufted vetch is one of the most widespread and abundant, but bush vetch and common vetch are also common.

Each leaf is divided into 6–15 pairs of narrow leaflets. Branched tendrils grow from the tip of each leaf. Up to six seeds grow in a long, 20-millimetre seed pod.

► *Tufted vetch has spikes of bluish-purple, slightly drooping flowers.*

Agrimony

Scientific name: *Agrimonia eupatoria*
Height: 30–60 cm
Family: rose
Flowering months: June–August

Agrimony is a stiff, upright plant that is common in dry grassy places, such as roadsides, banks of hedges and chalk grasslands. Most of the leaves grow low down on the stems. Both the stems and the leaves are hairy. The leaves are divided into leaflets of different sizes. There are 3–6 pairs of larger leaflets, and between them a pair of much smaller leaflets. Many small yellow flowers grow in clusters on a long stem. Seeds grow inside fruits covered in tiny hooks, which cling to fur, feathers and clothing.

◄ *The small yellow flowers of agrimony grow on a tall upright stem.*

Wild strawberry

Scientific name: *Fragaria vesca*
Height: 5–30 cm
Family: rose
Flowering months: April–July

► *These wild strawberries are much smaller than those for sale in shops, but their flavour is very strong.*

Just like a smaller version of cultivated strawberries, the wild strawberry plant has stems that arch over the ground, growing into new plants at the tips. The leaves are divided into three toothed leaflets. Flowers grow in sprays of only a few blooms. The fruits, or strawberries, of this plant are much smaller than those on sale in the shops, but they have a very strong flavour.

Silverweed

Scientific name: *Potentilla anserina*
Height: 5–25 cm
Family: rose
Flowering months: May–August

Although silverweed grows low on the ground, its leaves seldom standing upright, its creeping stems can be up to 80 centimetres long. Since many new plants grow from these stems, silverweed can form dense patches on dry, grassy places, wasteland, fields or roadsides.

The leaves are divided into 7–12 pairs of toothed leaflets. The underside and often the upper surface of the leaf is covered with silky, silvery hairs, which gave this plant its name. Its single yellow flowers grow on leafless stems.

◄ *Silverweed is a low-growing plant with creeping stems.*

Dog rose

Scientific name: *Rosa canina*
Height: 1–3 metres
Family: rose
Flowering months: June–July

Many wild roses grow in hedgerows. Dog rose is the most common of these roses. Its arching woody stems scramble over other hedgerow shrubs. These stems bear many stout, curved prickles, which help the stems hook on to other plants and use them for support. Together with brambles, they turn a hedge into a painful barrier!

Dog rose flowers are an attractive sight in early summer, and are a feast for insects gathering nectar and pollen. The fruits are hard woody nutlets. They are tightly packed inside round or oval, fleshy red 'rosehips', which are swollen tips of the flower stem.

Burnet rose is a similar plant to dog rose, but it grows into a low thicket of prickly stems. Burnet rose is usually found near the sea. The flowers are creamy white, and the small, round hips are purplish-black.

▲ *These dog rose flowers are white, but others are pink.*

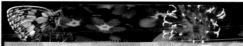
Inside each rosehip there is a hard nutlet surrounded by fibres, which irritate human and animal skin. In the past, rosehips were used to make itching powder!

Bramble

Scientific name: *Rubus fruticosus*
Height: over 2 metres
Family: rose
Flowering months: May–September

Brambles are fiercely prickly, as anyone who has tried to pick its fruits (the sweet, juicy blackberries) will know. The prickly stems of bramble either grow flat over the ground, or arch over other shrubs and small trees to a height of 2 metres or more. Brambles start to flower in mid-summer. Their pink-petalled flowers attract bees, flies and butterflies gathering pollen. Brambles that start to flower as early as May will produce their first blackberries in early August, but most blackberries are ripe in late August and September. Blackberries that ripen later in October do not taste as good.

▲ *Blackberries are green at first. Then they turn yellow, then red and finally black. They are only ripe when they are black.*

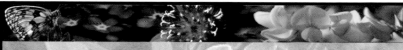
The bramble's ripe blackberries are a feast for blackbirds, thrushes and other birds, wasps and, of course, people! There are usually enough wild brambles to provide blackberries for puddings, jams or even blackberry wine, as long as you have the patience to pick them.

15

Meadowsweet

Scientific name: *Filipendula ulmaria*
Height: 60–120 cm
Family: rose
Flowering months: June–September

◀ *The tiny flowers of meadowsweet are strongly scented.*

Large clumps of meadowsweet grow in damp places beside ponds, or along river and canal banks. The leaves at the base of the plant are divided into pairs of unevenly toothed leaflets, separated by pairs of much smaller leaflets. The leaves higher up the stem are much smaller, with fewer leaflets. The flower head is branched, with each branchlet bearing a spray of tiny, fluffy white flowers.

▲ *Purple loosestrife can grow into large clumps beside rivers, streams or ponds.*

Purple loosestrife

Scientific name: *Lythrum salicaria*
Height: 60–120 cm
Family: loosestrife
Flowering months: June–August

Like meadowsweet, purple loosestrife grows well beside ponds and rivers. It is also found in fens and marshes. In a good location, this stiff-stemmed, greyish-green, hairy plant can spread itself rapidly. The leaves are lance-shaped, and grow all the way up the stem, to just below the spike of reddish-purple flowers.

Rosebay willowherb

Scientific name: *Chamerion angustifolium*
Height: 30–120 cm
Family: willowherb
Flowering months: June–September

Rosebay willowherb used to be quite uncommon, growing on loose rocky slopes, but in the past 100 years or so, it has become common and widespread on dry patches of wasteland. It became a characteristic plant around bombed land sites after the Second World War, because the ruined buildings resembled the dry rocks of its natural habitat.

Rosebay willowherb has tall, straight stems, with lots of lance-shaped leaves. Many pinkish-purple flowers grow in a loose spike at the top of each stem. The fruit is a slender, upright capsule which splits to release fluffy, airborne seeds. Rosebay willowherb also spreads using creeping underground stems.

▶ *Each rosebay willowherb flower has four petals, the upper two of which are wider than the lower two.*

▼ *In the right place, rosebay willow-herb can form a large patch.*

Cow parsley

Scientific name: *Anthriscus sylvestris*
Height: 60–100 cm
Family: carrot
Flowering months: April–June

Cow parsley grows along hedgerows, beside fields and on wasteland. It has flat heads of tiny white flowers, which grow in clusters at the ends of slender stems arranged like the spokes of an umbrella. Botanists call this type of flower head an umbel, which comes from the Latin word *umbella*, meaning sunshade. The leaves are divided three times into small leaflets.

Cow parsley is one of the most common members of the carrot family. It is related to carrots, parsnips, fennel and true parsley, which are all edible members of the same large family. Unlike these tasty and nutritious relatives, cow parsley and some of its other relatives are not good to

▲ *The lacy flower heads of cow parsley are a sure sign that summer is on its way.*

eat, and many other members of the carrot family are actually very poisonous. The poisonous species can be dangerously difficult to distinguish from their edible relatives, so it is never wise to eat any member of this family that you find in the wild.

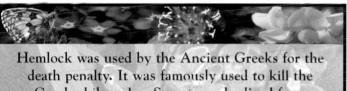

Hemlock was used by the Ancient Greeks for the death penalty. It was famously used to kill the Greek philosopher Socrates, who lived from 469–399 BC. Socrates was sentenced to death in Athens at the age of seventy, for challenging the philosophy and politics of the Athenians.

Hemlock

Scientific name: *Conium maculatum*
Height: up to 2 metres
Family: carrot
Flowering months: June–July

Hemlock is a very poisonous member of the carrot family. It has flat heads of tiny white flowers and finely divided, 'lacy' leaves. Other poisonous members of the carrot family include fool's parsley, hemlock water dropwort and cowbane. When bruised, the leaves of hemlock water dropwort have an unpleasant smell. Hemlock prefers damp soil, growing in suitable patches of wasteland, beside ditches or beside roads.

Giant hogweed is an unmistakable relative of hemlock. It is an enormous wild flower, growing up to 5 metres tall beside rivers. Originally from south-west Asia, giant hogweed was planted in Britain for its curiosity value. Be careful not to touch it – the sap can cause painful blisters.

◀ *Hemlock has more lacy looking leaves than cow parsley and unlike cow parsley, it has purple spots on its tall stems.*

Goosegrass

Scientific name: *Galium aparine*
Height: 15–120 cm
Family: bedstraw
Flowering months: May–September

Goosegrass, or cleavers as it is sometimes called, clings to clothes with its sharp prickles. The prickles grow pointing downwards along the plant's square stems and edges of the leaves. Since the stems are weak, the prickles help the plant scramble over stronger plants or walls for support.

Goosegrass leaves are narrow and are arranged in whorls of 6–8 along the stem. You have to look closely to see the clusters of tiny white flowers. The fruits are much more noticeable. Each has two rounded lobes, both covered with tiny hooked bristles, so that they cling to fur, feathers or clothing just like the stems and leaves.

► *These goosegrass stems look sturdy, but they are unable to support their own weight.*

Teasel

Scientific name: *Dipsacus fullonum*
Height: 50–200 cm
Family: teasel
Flowering months: July–August

If you find a teasel, look at it carefully before you touch it. The stiff square stems are very prickly, and underneath the leaves, running along the centre is another row of sturdy, hooked prickles. The leaves are arranged up the stem in pairs. At the base of the plant they are joined together to form a cup, which collects rainwater for the plant.

The teasel's flower head is cylindrical in shape and made up of a mass of tiny, lilac-coloured flowers, each enclosed in a bristly cup. In late summer goldfinches can be seen clinging to these flower heads, pecking out the seeds. A variety of teasel that has a flower head with very stiff, hooked bristles was once specially grown and used by wool spinners and cloth makers.

◄ *Teasel flowers are tiny and open in rings around the flower head, starting at the base and slowly moving to the top.*

Biting stonecrop

Scientific name: *Sedum acre*
Height: 2–10 cm
Family: stonecrop
Flowering months: May–July

Stonecrops can grow in extremely dry places, among rocks, on walls, or in very dry grassland, waste ground or sand dunes. They survive by storing water in their swollen leaves.

Biting stonecrop, sometimes known as wall pepper, has creeping stems which spread to make a mat. Its fleshy oval leaves are only 3–5 millimetres long and are often tinged red. In flower, biting stonecrop is a mass of star-shaped, bright yellow flowers.

▲ *When biting stonecrop is in full flower, there are so many bright yellow flowers that they completely hide the leaves.*

Harebell

▲ *The bell shape of the harebell's flowers protects the pollen from rain.*

Scientific name: *Campanula rotundifolia*
Height: 15–50 cm
Family: bellflower
Flowering months: July–September

The delicate harebell grows on dry, chalky grassland. It has slender, upright stems and leaves of two different shapes. The leaves that grow at the base of the plant are almost round, whereas those that grow on the stem are long and narrow. The lilac flowers are bell-shaped with five lobes. Seeds grow inside a rounded capsule. When they are ripe, the seeds are released through tiny holes. The flowers and the seed capsules nod gently in the breeze, which may help to shake out the ripe seeds.

Heather

Scientific name: *Calluna vulgaris*
Height: up to 60 cm
Family: heather
Flowering months: July–September

▶ *Lots of small rose-purple flowers grow up the stems of heather.*

Heather is a small woody shrub, with many thin, branched stems. It can grow more or less upright, or sprawl over the ground making a dense carpet of springy twigs. The small leaves are pressed closely along the stems so that they look like green scales. Even though each individual flower is only about 3.5 millimetres long, when blossoming heather covers large areas of heathland or hillside it is a striking sight.

Daisy

Scientific name: *Bellis perennis*
Height: 4–12 cm
Family: daisy
Flowering months: March–October

Daisies scatter themselves over the short turf of lawns, to the annoyance of many gardeners! Their leaves are oval and are arranged in a flat rosette on the ground. The 'flower', which grows at the top of the stem, is actually a head made up of many single flowers, or florets. There are two different types of floret in each daisy flower head: those in the centre of the head are yellow and tubular, called disc florets. Surrounding these is a fringe of ray florets, each with a white or pink-tipped petal.

▲ *Daisies were named after the Old English words for 'day's eye' because the flowers close at night and open in the day.*

Ox-eye daisy

Scientific name: *Leucanthemum vulgare*
Height: 20–70 cm
Family: daisy
Flowering months: June–August

Like its smaller cousin, the ox-eye daisy has a flower head made up of a central disc of small yellow disc florets and an outer circle of white-petalled ray florets. Ox-eye daisy flower heads can grow up to 5 centimetres across. Unlike its smaller relative, it has lobed leaves growing from its stems. The leaves at the base of the plant are oval, with bluntly toothed edges.

▲ *Ox-eye daisies grow in grassy places such as meadows, embankments and hedgerows. They prefer chalky or fertile soil.*

Yarrow

Scientific name: *Achillea millefolium*
Height: 8–60 cm
Family: daisy
Flowering months: June–August

Yarrow is a common and distinctive plant, which grows in meadows, gardens, waysides, hedgerows and other grassy places. The long green leaves are divided 2–3 times into many tiny narrow leaflets, which gives the plant a feathery appearance. When crushed, these leaves give off a scent that is pleasant to humans, but may put off some plant-eating insects.

▶ *Yarrow can have pure white, pinkish-white or pink flowers.*

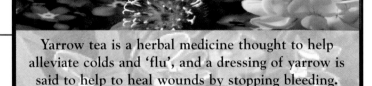

Yarrow tea is a herbal medicine thought to help alleviate colds and 'flu', and a dressing of yarrow is said to help to heal wounds by stopping bleeding.

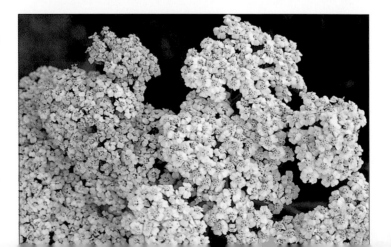

Common ragwort

Scientific name: *Senecio jacobaea*
Height: 30–150 cm
Family: daisy
Flowering months: June–October

Common ragwort is a sturdy plant that grows quickly on pastures, roadsides and wastelands. Its stiff, furrowed stems bear many narrow leaves. At the base of the plant is a rosette of leaves with broader lobes. Clusters of yellow, daisy-like flowers grow at the tops of the branched stems. Each seed is encased in a tough fruit topped with a plume of cottony hairs. The hairs help to spread the seed by keeping it airborne.

Ragwort has an unpleasant scent when bruised, which is the plant's way of letting animals know that it is poisonous. It is especially dangerous to grazing animals, such as cattle and horses, so it is a pest to livestock farmers, especially since it is difficult to destroy completely. The caterpillars of the cinnabar moth, however, are not affected by the ragwort's poison when they eat the plant. In fact, they use it as their own method of self-defence by becoming poisonous themselves.

▲ *Ragwort's yellow flowers may be pretty, but the plant is a serious weed of pastures and meadows.*

Young dandelion leaves can be eaten cooked, or raw in salads. Wine can also be made from dandelion flowers.

▼ *Each single-seeded dandelion fruit, with its parachute of hairs, snaps from the old flower head and blows away in the wind.*

Dandelion

Scientific name: *Taraxacum officinale*
Height: 5–40 cm
Family: daisy
Flowering months: March–October

Together with buttercups and daisies, the dandelion is one of our most familiar and easily recognized wild flowers. It springs up almost everywhere – in gardens, parks, playing fields and roadsides.

The word 'dandelion' comes from the French word *dents de lion*, meaning 'lion's teeth', because the plant's long lobed leaves look like large teeth. Each flower head is made up of many ray florets with yellow petals. The stem that bears each flower oozes a white milky sap when it is cut. When it is in fruit, the whole flower head is a round mass of small, single-seeded fruits, each with a crown of stiff white hairs. This is sometimes called the dandelion's 'clock'. The hairs help the seeds blow away in the wind, or you can pick them and blow them away yourself!

Spear thistle

Scientific name: *Cirsium vulgare*
Height: 30–150 cm
Family: daisy
Flowering months: July–October

The spear thistle is a tall plant with flower heads arranged in dense clusters at the tips of branches. The leaves, stems and green bases of the flower heads are all clothed in fiercely sharp spines. The flower heads are roughly oval in shape, with many pinkish-purple florets. Like many other members of the daisy family, the ripe seeds are spread by the wind, kept airborne by a parachute of cottony hairs.

There are many other kinds of thistle, including the dwarf and marsh thistle. They are all fiercely spiny, as anyone who has ever brushed against one, or sat on their leaves, will know. Their spines stop animals such as rabbits, deer, horses and cattle from eating them.

▶ *When the flowers have died, this flower head will turn into a fluffy seed ball, like the dandelion.*

Great burdock

Scientific name: *Arctium lappa*
Height: 90–130 cm
Family: daisy
Flowering months: July–September

Great burdock is a sturdy, bushy plant found on wasteland, hedgerows and clearings near footpaths and watercourses. It has large heart-shaped leaves and a number of branched stems, with grooves running along their length. The flower heads are round-shaped, with tiny purple florets almost hidden inside a cup of scale-like bracts. Each bract has a long stiff tip drawn out into a hook. When the seeds are ripe, these hooks catch on to the fur of passing animals and the whole fruit head is carried off. The hooks also snag on to clothing, so if you brush against a burdock while out walking, you will have to pull off the clinging 'burrs'.

◀ *The hooked bracts surrounding this flower head will help to spread the seeds by clinging to the fur of passing animals.*

Primrose

Scientific name: *Primula vulgaris*
Height: 8–20 cm
Family: primrose
Flowering months: January–May

A hedge bank or woodland clearing is a lovely sight in spring when primroses come into bloom. Primrose flowers are yellowish-white and grow singly on slender stems. The bases of the petals are enclosed in hairy sepals, joined together in a tube shape. Each of the five petals has a deep notch at its tip. The toothed leaves are oval to oblong in shape, rather wrinkled in appearance and with hairs covering the lower surface. The leaf blade tapers into a short stem.

▲ *Primrose flowers rise up from a dense clump of leaves.*

Creeping jenny

Scientific name: *Lysimachia nummularia*
Height: about 5 cm
Family: daisy
Flowering months: May–July

This creeping plant may be only a few centimetres high, but the trailing stems are up to 60 centimetres long. Pairs of round leaves grow close together along the stems, speckled with tiny black dots. The flowers have five, slightly cupped, yellow petals, and the lobes of the petals are also sprinkled with black dots. Creeping jenny grows in damp woodland clearings, banks of hedges and other moist, slightly shaded, grassy places.

▲ *Creeping jenny grows low on the ground.*

Scarlet pimpernel

Scientific name: *Anagallis arvensis*
Height: 5–20 cm
Family: daisy
Flowering months: May–October

Scarlet pimpernel likes to grow in soil that has been recently disturbed or broken up, so it is a common weed of fields of crops, gardens, roadsides or sand dunes. It has stems with four sides, which usually drape over the ground. The roughly oval leaves are arranged opposite each other, and their lower surface is speckled with black dots. The small flowers, each with five petals, are bright red, although occasionally they may be blue. Seeds develop inside a small round capsule.

▲ *Scarlet pimpernel flowers open at about 8.00 am and close again at about 3.00 pm. They also close in damp weather, re-opening when the sun comes out.*

Field forget-me-not

Scientific name: *Myosotis arvensis*
Height: 15–30 cm
Family: borage
Flowering months: April–September

▶ *The best time to spot field forget-me-nots is in May, when most of the flowers are open.*

Field forget-me-not, also called common forget-me-not, is another wild flower that grows as a weed in the garden, or in dry, sunny places beside paths or in fields. When in flower, it is easy to spot because although each flower is tiny (no more than 4 millimetres wide), the flowers grow in clusters. The flowers are pale blue, with yellow centres. The leaves and stems are slightly hairy.

The wood forget-me-not is similar to the field forget-me-not, but it has a blue-and-yellow central flower, and grows in damp woodlands. Water forget-me-nots is also similar, but it grows in wet places beside water and in ditches.

Forget-me-nots have appeared in legends as a symbol of friendship and love. In one German legend, they were the last words said by a lover to his sweetheart before he drowned trying to pick one for her.

Viper's bugloss

Scientific name: *Echium vulgare*
Height: 30–90 cm
Family: borage
Flowering months: June–September

This stiff, upright plant, also known as blue thistle, has pale stems covered with very prickly hairs. The leaves are long and narrow. The funnel-shaped flowers are reddish at first, but turn a deep purple colour when they are open. The flowers are arranged in sprays up the stem. Each flower has stamens that are much longer than the petals.

▲ *People used to think viper's bugloss cured viper bites.*

Common comfrey

Scientific name: *Symphytum officinale*
Height: 30–120 cm
Family: borage
Flowering months: May–July

▶ *Common comfrey grows in large clumps with tubular flowers.*

Common comfrey is a large plant, with stems and leaves clothed in bristly hairs, so the whole plant is rough to touch. The leaves are roughly oval in shape. The leaves growing higher up do not have stalks, while the leaves growing at the base of the plant have stalks. The coiled sprays of the tubular flowers are creamy white, pink or purple. Common comfrey grows in damp places beside streams, rivers and ponds.

Field bindweed

Scientific name: *Convolvulus arvensis*
Height: 20–75 cm
Family: convolvulus
Flowering months: June–September

Field bindweed, like other members of the convolvulus family, has stems that twine and twist around other plants. Without support it creeps over the ground because the stem is too weak to support the plant's weight. The leaves are oval or arrow-shaped. The funnel-shaped flowers can be almost white, pink, or pink and white. They do not last very long and close in dull weather.

Field bindweed grows in light, dry soil that has recently been broken up or cultivated. It is a common weed of farmland and annoying to farmers. It is very difficult to eradicate because the roots can extend 2 metres or more into the earth.

▲ *The delicate flowers of field bindweed close in dull, damp weather and open again when the sun comes out.*

Hedge bindweed

Scientific name: *Calystegia sepium*
Height: up to 3 metres
Family: convolvulus
Flowering months: July–September

Hedge bindweed is a much sturdier plant than field bindweed, and will climb to greater heights. It can cover a whole bush or fence with its twining stems and large, arrow-shaped leaves. The flowers close at night and open again at dawn. The seeds of bindweeds grow in small capsules, which split to release them when they are ripe.

Hedge bindweed grows on railway embankments, farmland and waste ground. It is a common garden weed. Although its large flowers are attractive, its habit of smothering other plants make it very unpopular with gardeners. It spreads rapidly using creeping underground stems. These snap if you try to pull them up, and even a small piece left behind in the soil can grow into a new bindweed plant.

◀ *Hedge bindweed flowers are large white funnels, which are very thin and delicate.*

Bittersweet

Scientific name: *Solanum dulcamara*
Height: 30–200 cm
Family: potato
Flowering months: June–September

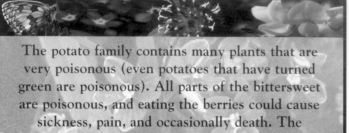

The potato family contains many plants that are very poisonous (even potatoes that have turned green are poisonous). All parts of the bittersweet are poisonous, and eating the berries could cause sickness, pain, and occasionally death. The bittersweet's relative, the deadly nightshade, is even more dangerous. Just five ripe, purple berries could kill a child.

▲ *Bittersweet's flowers can range from purple to pale blue.*

Bittersweet, or woody nightshade, is a climbing plant with woody stems. It grows in hedgerows, wasteland and on shingle beaches. The leaves vary in shape. Some leaves are oval, while others are heart or arrow-shaped, with 2–4 lobes at their base. The flowers are arranged in branched clusters and, in the centre of each flower, the stamens are joined together to make a yellow 'cone'. In late summer the plant produces bright red berries.

Foxglove

Scientific name: *Digitalis purpurea*
Height: 50–150 cm
Family: figwort
Flowering months: June–September

The foxglove is a distinctive plant, named because its flowers look a little like the fingers of a glove. Its tall spires of purple 'bells' are arranged up a sturdy, stiff stem. Each drooping flower has a lower lip, and inside there are often darker spots or rings. Bumble bees crawl right inside these bells to reach the nectar. The seeds grow inside capsules, which open along small slits near the tip. Foxglove leaves are oval-shaped, hairy and greyish-green, with a wrinkled appearance.

The whole foxglove plant is bitter-tasting and poisonous, but it is useful too. In 1785, an English doctor called William Withering discovered that it helped in the treatment of certain diseases. Today, a number of valuable medicines that are used to treat some heart conditions are still made from the foxglove's leaves.

◀ *The foxglove's bell-shaped flowers grow up one side of a tall stem.*

Great mullein

Scientific name: *Verbascum thapsus*
Height: 30–200 cm
Family: figwort
Flowering months: June–September

Great mullein is a tall, upright plant that grows beside roads, and in dry stony places such as wasteland and sunny banks. Like its relative, the foxglove, bell-shaped flowers grow up tall stems. All parts of the lance-shaped leaves, stem and flower buds are densely covered in soft white hairs. This makes the whole plant pale green and very soft to touch.

▶ *Great mullein's tall spikes of flowers make it a distinctive plant.*

▲ *Each common figwort flower is small and purplish-brown.*

◀ *Common figwort has small flowers compared to its relatives, the foxglove and great mullein.*

Common figwort

Scientific name: *Scrophularia nodosa*
Height: 40–80 cm
Family: figwort
Flowering months: June–September

Common figwort has branched, square stems. The leaves are roughly oval in shape, with edges that are coarsely and unevenly toothed. At the top of the stems, the flowers are arranged in a loosely branched flower head. The petals are joined into a short roundish tube drawn out into a lip at the top. Figwort flowers are pollinated by wasps. The wasps feed on their nectar. Common figwort grows in damp places in woodland clearings, hedgerows and beside water.

Ivy-leaved toadflax

Scientific name: *Cymbalaria muralis*
Stem length: 10–80 cm
Family: figwort
Flowering months: May–September

▶ *Ivy-leaved toadflax grows quickly along creeping stems.*

Ivy-leaved toadflax has many stems, which creep over the ground or hang down over rocks and walls. The leaves are kidney-shaped, with five lobes. Both the stems and the leaves are often tinged purple. The violet-coloured flowers have two flat petals, or lips, at the front, with a yellow patch above the lower lip. At the back of each flower is a short spur.

Germander speedwell

Scientific name: *Veronica chamaedrys*
Height: 20–40 cm
Family: figwort
Flowering months: March–July

Germander speedwell grows in woodlands and grassy areas, hedges and embankments. It has hairy, almost triangular, toothed leaves and clusters of bright blue flowers, with small heart-shaped seed capsules. Its relative, the common field speedwell, is a weed of cultivated land. It is similar to germander speedwell but it has oval rather than triangular leaves and the lower petal is smaller and much paler than the others.

► *Each germander speedwell blossom has four bright-blue petals.*

White deadnettle

Scientific name: *Lamium album*
Height: 20–60 cm
Family: mint
Flowering months: April–November

White deadnettle grows in woodlands, waysides and hedgerows. It has oval or heart-shaped hairy leaves that are coarsely toothed. At first sight, the leaves look just like those of stinging nettle (see page 31), which is how this, and related plants, get their name. Like other plants in the mint family, white deadnettle has square stems. Each flower is tube-shaped and ends in lobes, the upper one of which is hooded.

Red deadnettle is similar to white deadnettle, but it has purplish-pink flowers and the upper leaves are flushed with reddish purple. It is a common weed of gardens and cultivated ground. Another similar species, but one that prefers shady banks and woodland edges, is the yellow archangel, which has whorls of bright yellow flowers.

◄ *The white deadnettle's creamy white flowers grow in whorls around the stem.*

Self-heal

Scientific name: *Prunella vulgaris*
Height: 5–30 cm
Family: mint
Flowering months: June–November

► *On lawns, self-heal grows in a short mat.*

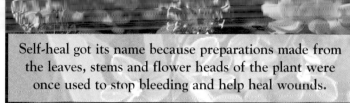

If you notice patches of a purple-flowered plant on your lawn or on a playing field, look at it closely. It may be self-heal, which grows into a mat short enough to escape the lawnmower. In woodland clearings and grassy wasteland self-heal grows taller, and the tubular, lipped flowers are easier to see. The leaves are oval and may have shallow teeth around the edges.

Self-heal got its name because preparations made from the leaves, stems and flower heads of the plant were once used to stop bleeding and help heal wounds.

Skullcap

Scientific name: *Scutellaria galericulata*
Height: 15–50 cm
Family: mint
Flowering months: June–September

Skullcap is a fairly common plant that grow on the edges of streams and in damp, grassy places. Its flowers are easy to miss because they are almost hidden among the lance-shaped leaves. The flowers are a violet-blue colour and arranged in pairs up the stems. They are slender and tube-shaped. Lesser skullcap is a similar plant, but it is smaller with pink flowers.

◄ *Look for skullcap beside ditches and streams.*

Wood sage

Scientific name: *Teucrium scorodonia*
Height: 15–30 cm
Family: mint
Flowering months: July–September

Wood sage stems are stiff and woody, especially near the base. The almost heart-shaped leaves are hairy and have a very wrinkled appearance. The flowers are narrow, pale green and tube-shaped, with a long lower lip that bends backwards. Two maroon pollen sacs stick out from the top of the flower. The flowers are all arranged along one side of a spike, facing the same way. Wood sage is a common wild flower of sandy heathlands, but it also grows in dry grasslands and woods.

▲ *Wood sage grows in clumps of upright stems.*

Greater plantain

Scientific name: *Plantago major*
Height: 10–35 cm
Family: plantain
Flowering months: June–October

The large oval leaves of greater plantain are all in a rosette at the base of the plant. Along the upper part of each tall, unbranched flower stem is a spike of tiny flowers. The whitish petals are tiny, but it is easy to see the stamens – these are long and stick well out from the flowers. Ribwort plantain is a relative of greater plantain. It has long narrow leaves and a shorter oval spike of flowers. Both these plantains are wind-pollinated. They grow in open, grassy places.

◀ *The leaves of greater plantain often lie almost flat on the ground, but the flower stem stands tall and upright.*

Curled dock

Scientific name: *Rumex crispus*
Height: 50–100 cm
Family: dock
Flowering months: June–October

▶ *Curled dock is a troublesome weed of pastures and farmland. It flourishes on open disturbed ground and can also be found on shingle beaches.*

Curled dock has upright stems that are stiff, thick and slightly ridged. The lance-shaped leaves, which are up to 30 centimetres long, have wavy or curled edges. The flowers are small and each has three, greenish petals. They are arranged in dense, closely-packed whorls.

Sun spurge

Scientific name: *Euphorbia helioscopa*
Height: 10–50 cm
Family: spurge
Flowering months: May–August

Sun spurge, like all members of the spurge family, is poisonous. It oozes a milky white sap when it is cut, which can irritate human and animal skin.

The leaves grow all the way up the stems of the plant, each one broadest towards the tip and tapering towards the stem. When in flower, whorls of green bracts that look like leaves surround the flower clusters. The seeds grow in a rounded, three-lobed capsule.

◀ *Sun spurge has tiny yellowish-green flowers surrounded by four oval structures, called glands.*

Stinging nettle

Scientific name: *Urtica dioica*
Height: 30–150 cm
Family: nettle
Flowering months: June–September

▶ *This stinging nettle is a male plant. It has long slender catkins of tiny greenish male flowers, which produce masses of pollen.*

Stinging nettle grows in large patches of stiff, upright stems. Dark green leaves are arranged in opposite pairs up each stem. The leaves are heart shaped and have coarsely toothed edges. As a way of protecting itself, the plant's leaves and stems are covered in sharp, brittle hairs, which inject tiny droplets of a painful stinging liquid when they are touched. These 'stings' may tingle and smart for up to a day, but they do no lasting harm.

The male and female flowers of the stinging nettle grow on separate plants. Both types of flower are very small and green. The male flowers are arranged in long, slender catkins, which hang in bunches among the leaves near the top of the stem. Female flowers are also arranged near the top of the stem, but they are arranged in much tighter clusters. Stinging nettles like to grow in rich, fertile soils of neglected gardens, or farmland.

Stinging nettles have been used as medicines since ancient times. Young nettle plants can be cooked and eaten like spinach. They are full of vitamins and minerals.

Mistletoe

Scientific name: *Viscum album*
Stem height: up to 1 metre
Family: mistletoe
Flowering months: February–April

The best time to see mistletoe growing is in winter, when leaves fall off most trees. This is because mistletoe does not grow in the ground. Instead, its seeds germinate on and grow into the branches of trees such as apple, lime, poplar and hawthorn. Mistletoe makes its own food by photosynthesis, like other green plants, but it takes all the water and nutrients it needs from the tree on which it is growing. Botanists call it a semi-parasite.

The mistletoe's stems and leaves are yellowish-green. Each stem branches many times, so that the whole plant can eventually grow into a loose, spherical shape up to 2 metres across. The separate male and female flowers are small and green, but the white berries are much more noticeable.

▲ *This tree's leaves have fallen, showing the yellowish-green mistletoe growing on its branches.*

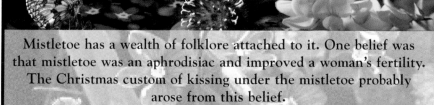

Mistletoe has a wealth of folklore attached to it. One belief was that mistletoe was an aphrodisiac and improved a woman's fertility. The Christmas custom of kissing under the mistletoe probably arose from this belief.

Himalayan balsam

Scientific name: *Impatiens glandulifera*
Height: 1–2 metres
Family: balsam
Flowering months: July–October

► *The Himalayan balsam is also called 'policeman's helmet' because of the shape of its pink and white flowers.*

Himalayan balsam is not native to Europe. As its name suggests, it comes from the slopes of the Himalayan mountains. It was brought to Britain and other European countries in about 1839 and was planted in gardens. However, it escaped from gardens and now grows well in the wild beside streams and rivers. It grows so fast that it has become a pest because it shades out smaller, native plants.

The Himalayan balsam's stems are thick and fleshy. Oval, toothed leaves grow in opposite pairs or whorls of three. The flowers are pink, purplish or white, and are arranged in sprays. Each flower has a tube-shaped base, with a hooded upper petal and two lower petals forming a lip. When the ripe seed capsule is touched, it explodes violently, shooting the seeds out in all directions.

Common spotted orchid

▼ *A dense spike of pink or white orchid flowers grows on a tall flower stem.*

Scientific name: *Dactylorhiza fuchsii*
Height: 25–50 cm
Family: orchid
Flowering months: June–August

This is the most common orchid in much of Britain and Ireland. It has narrow tapering leaves, which are distinctively blotched with dark spots. Common orchid flowers are tube-shaped, with a short spur pointing backwards. At the front of the tube there are two pink, wing-shaped sepals and a three-lobed lip. The lip of each flower is patterned with lines and dots.

There are many different kinds of orchids. The early purple orchid also has spotted leaves, but each flower has a long spur that points upward. Some orchids are extremely rare. Rarities such as the bee, lizard and fly orchid have flowers of the most bizarre appearance.

The vanilla orchid is a relative of the common spotted orchid. It grows throughout the tropics. It is used to produce vanilla flavouring, which is used in food and drink.

Common twayblade

► *Common twayblade has tiny green flowers that grow on a tall spike.*

Scientific name: *Listera ovata*
Height: 20–60 cm
Family: orchid
Flowering months: May–July

Common twayblade is a widespread orchid that grows in woodlands, moorlands and damp hedgerows, on chalky soils. Each plant has just one pair of leaves. These leaves are oval, with 3–5 distinct ribs. The greenish flowers grow on a slender spike. Each has a 'hood' of sepals and petals, and a long lip that is deeply notched.

Yellow flag

Scientific name: *Iris pseudacorus*
Height: 40–150 cm
Family: iris
Flowering months: June–August

► *You cannot miss yellow flag when it is in full flower, especially as it often grows in large patches.*

Yellow flag grows in large clumps beside streams, ponds, marshes and other wet places. It has tall sword-shaped leaves which grow from a thick, creeping stem. The stem may be underground or just on the surface. The leaves are bluish green, with a distinct mid-rib. Each flower stem has 2–3 large yellow flowers. The structure of the flowers is quite complex. Three floral parts are broad and curve downwards, and three are smaller, narrower and curve upwards. The seed capsules are cylindrical, narrowing at both ends. When ripe, the capsules split into three parts, each part containing two rows of tightly packed, reddish-brown seeds.

Ramsons

Scientific name: *Allium ursinum*
Height: 25–45 cm
Family: lily
Flowering months: April–June

Ramsons, or wild garlic, has bright green leaves that smell strongly of garlic. The upright three-sided flower stem grows a rounded head of 6–20 flowers. The flowers look as through they have six white petals, but three of these are actually sepals.

Ramsons often grows in large patches in damp parts of woodlands, banks of hedges or shaded corners in wet meadows. It is an attractive sight when in full flower. After a shower of rain, the garlicky smell fills the air.

► *Ramsons can cover large areas of a woodland floor.*

WATER PLANTS

Some wild flowers can only grow in water, or where the ground is always extremely damp. These plants are never found in drier places. Some, such as the river water crowfoot, have all their leaves underwater. Others, such as the white water lily, have leaves that float on the surface. The pond water crowfoot has both submerged leaves and floating leaves, which are different in appearance. Yet other water plants, such as reed-mace, grow with just their roots permanently submerged.

Since the water supports much of the weight of the plant, those that are entirely submerged often have succulent, juicy stems. There is no waxy layer covering these, so nutrients and dissolved gases such as carbon dioxide and oxygen can be absorbed through the stems as well as through the roots. These plants have many air spaces in their stems and leaves, which help to keep the leaves afloat. When removed from the water, these plants flop and quickly dry out.

White water lily

Scientific name: *Nymphaea alba*
Stem length: up to 3 metres
Family: water-lily
Flowering months: June–September

The thick, dark green leaves of this water lily are almost circular, deeply split to the point where the leaf blade joins the stem. The large flowers are 10–20 centimetres wide and are held up just above the water. Each flower has 20–25 white petals, which surround numerous yellow stamens.

◀ *White water lily roots are anchored in the mud at the bottom of a pond, lake or slow-moving river.*

Bogbean

Scientific name: *Menyanthes trifoliata*
Stem length: 10–35 cm
Family: bogbean
Flowering months: April–June

Bogbean prefers the shallower water at the edges of ponds, lakes and rivers. It will also grow in the wetter parts of marshes and bogs. The leaves are divided into three oval leaflets. The leaves and the flower heads are held well above the surface of the water. The flowers are arranged in stiff upright sprays. They are white flushed with pink, and each of the five petals is deeply fringed.

▶ *The floating stems of bogbean soon spread to cover the whole surface of a pond with new leafy shoots.*

Bulrush

Scientific name: *Typha latifolia*
Height: 1.5–3 metres
Family: reed mace
Flowering months: July–August

Bulrush, or reed-mace, is one of the most noticeable water plants. It spreads through the water at the edges of ponds, lakes and slow-flowing rivers. It has sword-shaped leaves that stand stiffly upright, often taller than the flower stem. At the top of each plant, the tiny yellow male flowers are arranged close together in a slender, tail-like spike. Immediately below these, the equally tiny, reddish-brown female flowers are clustered densely together to make a thick brown cylinder that is fuzzy to the touch. The following spring, this 'cylinder' splits open to release an enormous amount of fluffy seeds.

◀ *Bulrush is an easy water plant to identify. The flower spike lasts all winter, until it breaks up to release its seeds in spring.*

Common duckweed

Scientific name: *Lemna minor*
Frond: 1.5-4.0 mm wide
Family: duckweed
Flowering months: June–July

Duckweed is a common sight on garden ponds, canals and other still water, but it doesn't look like a flowering plant because it hardly ever has flowers. A tiny duckweed plant does not even have leaves. It has just rounded, green, pad-like 'fronds', which float on the surface. Each frond has one thin root, which dangles down into the water. The extremely small flowers are seldom formed. Instead, duckweed spreads mostly by growing new fronds at the edges of old fronds. Duckweed plants can quickly cover the entire surface of a pond so that it looks like a solid surface.

▶ *Tiny duckweed plants can completely cover the surface of the pond. Here you can see the pale green duckweed fronds as well as dark red fronds of the Azolla fern.*

WOODLAND FLOWERS

Woodlands are sheltered and have rich fertile soil but, when their leaves are open, the tall trees cast a deep shade on to the ground below. Plants need light to grow properly, so many of the wild flowers seen in woodlands are at their best in the spring, before the trees are in leaf. By growing leaves and flowers early in the year, while the light can still reach them, woodland plants such as bluebells and wood anemones can make enough food to set seed and store food reserves in bulbs or underground stems that will last until the following spring. By the time summer arrives, the leaves of these plants have died and there is no sign of them except the ripening fruits.

Other woodland wild flowers manage to get enough light by scrambling up taller shrubs and saplings. Honeysuckle and ivy are good examples. Honeysuckle climbs using long, arching stems that may twist around each other to form a rope, and ivy climbs using tiny root-like suckers that cling tightly to the bark of trees.

▶ *Each bluebell flower is just like a little bell hanging from a central flower stem.*

▼ *Carpets of bluebells in a woodland are a special attraction of a British springtime.*

Bluebell

Scientific name: *Hyacinthoides non-scripta*
Height: 20–50 cm
Family: lily
Flowering months: April–June

In May, bluebells are in full flower, covering vast areas of the woodland floor in a sea of blue. The bluebell is one of the specialities of the British countryside, and many people's favourite wild flower. Bluebell leaves are narrow and glossy green. They grow upright at first and then fall sideways, so that the taller flower stem is exposed. The flowers are drooping blue 'bells', arranged in curved sprays. They are sweetly scented. Bluebell seeds are black and grow in a capsule.

Ground ivy

Scientific name: *Glechoma hederacea*
Height: 10–25 cm
Family: mint
Flowering months: March–September

Ground ivy can be found flowering in woodland glades all summer, creeping over the ground. It is not related to true ivy, which can climb tree trunks. Ground ivy has square stems and kidney-shaped leaves. The leaves and stems are covered with soft hairs and are often tinged with purple. They have a strong, aromatic smell when crushed. The flowers are arranged in clusters, all facing in the same direction. Each has a tube-shaped base, with spots on the lower lip.

▶ *Ground ivy has purple, tube-shaped flowers.*

Honeysuckle

Scientific name: *Lonicera periclymenum*
Height: up to 6 metres
Family: honeysuckle
Flowering months: June–October

Honeysuckle has oval, bluish-green leaves arranged in pairs opposite each other. The flowers grow in clusters at the tips of short stems. Each flower has a long tube-shaped 'throat', with curled upper and lower lips. The stamens and upper part of the carpel stick out from the flower, so that visiting insects have to brush against them to reach the droplet of nectar at the base of the tube. Honeysuckle has a sweet, strong fragrance that attracts insects. This scent is strongest in the evening, when hawkmoths are active. The fruits are bright red, shiny berries which provide a feast for birds.

▲ Honeysuckle's clear red berries are harmless to people, but are best left for the birds to eat.

◄ Honeysuckle flowers are trumpet-shaped and have a sweet fragrance.

Wood anemone

Scientific name: *Anemone nemorosa*
Height: 6–30 cm
Family: buttercup
Flowering months: March–May

The delicate, deeply-lobed leaves of the wood anemone start to appear in late February, and the six-petalled white or pinkish-white flowers can be seen from March to May. These starry flowers only open when the sun shines on them, closing as evening falls and opening again the next day. Like bluebells, wood anemones can carpet large areas of the woodland floor. Their seeds grow in a round drooping head of small nutlets.

▶ Each wood anemone flower has six delicate, white or pinkish petals.

SEASIDE FLOWERS

At the back of every beach there is often a strip of sand, shingle or rocks out of reach of all but the stormiest seas. Here there is plenty of light, but no shelter from the wind or the scorching sun. The sand or pebbly shingle is loose and unstable, so rain water quickly drains through it. Only plants with special characteristics can flourish in these surroundings. Their roots and sometimes their spreading stems help to bind, or stabilize, the sand or shingle, which helps prevent it being blown away.

Seaside wild flowers need roots that are long enough to reach right down to water seeping from the land towards the sea. Thrift, which grows on rocks and shingle, has roots over a metre in length, while curled dock and sea holly, which live in sand, have roots up to 2.5 metres long. The leaves of seaside plants have thick waxy or fleshy leaves which prevent water loss and store water. The leaves have to be tough enough not to be damaged by the strong winds that sweep along coastal areas, and the salty spray blown off the sea.

▲ *When you find a mat of sea sandwort you will understand how it helps to hold the sand together and stop it blowing away.*

Sea sandwort

Scientific name: *Honkenya peploides*
Height: 5–25 cm
Family: pink
Flowering months: May–August

Sea sandwort is one of the first plants to grow on freshly blown sand. It has creeping stems with many branches, which spread across the sand to form a close mat. Sea sandwort has an extensive root system, and these roots, together with the closely spreading stems, help to bind the sand and prevent it blowing away.

Sea sandwort leaves are thick, fleshy and oval-shaped. They are arranged very close together opposite each other along the stems. The single flowers are either male or female, and both have five greenish-white petals. Its seeds grow inside a round capsule.

Yellow-horned poppy

Scientific name: *Glaucium maritimum*
Height: 30–90 cm
Family: poppy
Flowering months: June–September

Yellow-horned poppy is a robust plant, strong enough to survive battering by coastal winds laden with salt. It grows on the shingle beds that form at the back of some beaches. The leaves and stems are bluish-green and covered with rough hairs. The leaves at the base of the plant are deeply lobed. The upper leaves have more shallow lobes and clasp the stem. The seed capsule is a slender 'horn', which is 15–30 centimetres long.

▲ *Yellow-horned poppy's flowers make a bright splash of colour.*

Sea Holly

Scientific name: *Eryngium maritimum*
Height: 30–60 cm
Family: carrot
Flowering months: June–September

▼ *Sea holly is a bluish-green prickly plant that grows on sand at the back of beaches.*

Sea holly is usually seen growing on sand, although it also grows on shingle. Its pale blue-green appearance makes it easy to recognize. The roughly round leaves have 3–5 lobes, with white, spiny, toothed edges. It can be painful to step on this plant with bare feet when running over sand. The tiny blue flowers are tightly arranged in rounded flower heads, which are surrounded by spiny, leaf-like bracts.

Thrift

Scientific name: *Armeria maritima*
Height: 5–30 cm
Family: thrift
Flowering months: April–August

Thrift grows in tufts or clumps on rocky shores and cliffs. It will also grow on grasslands close to the sea. It needs plenty of light to grow. The leaves are narrow, grass-like and slightly fleshy. The flower stems grow taller than the leaves. Each bears a rounded cluster of pink flowers.

◀ *It is always amazing that thrift can grow so well on apparently bare rocks beside the sea. The roots grow deep into narrow splits in the rock to find water and nutrients.*

MOORLAND FLOWERS

Moorland is found in parts of the country that have a high rainfall and underlying rocks such as granite or sandstone. There are moors on the uplands and lowlands of Wales, Scotland, and parts of western and northern England. The soil on moorlands is low in nutrients and very often damp. Any trees are usually stunted and gnarled and, at first sight, a moor may seem rather bleak. But on closer inspection, you can find some interesting and attractive wild flowers.

In order to get more nutrients, some moorland wild flowers add insects to their diet. Sundews and butterworts both have sticky leaves that attract small flies. Once an insect lands, it cannot free itself. The leaves produce a liquid that digests the insect's body. This nourishing 'soup' is then absorbed by the plant.

Round-leaved sundew

Scientific name: *Drosera rotundifolia*
Height: 5–15 cm
Family: sundew
Flowering months: June–August

▶ *The remains of an insect can be seen trapped by the sticky leaf of this sundew plant. Nutrients from the insect's body will help the plant to make more seeds.*

The small round-leaved sundew is easy to spot because it has such a distinctive appearance. The leaves are arranged in a flat rosette. Each yellowish-green leaf is covered with red glands. At the tip of each gland glisten droplets of sticky liquid. When an insect gets stuck on these gluey droplets, the leaf folds up, trapping it still more. Sundew flowers are arranged in a spray at the top of a leafless stem. Each of these flowers usually has six white petals.

Great sundew and oblong-leaved sundew are similar to the round-leaved sundew, but they have different-shaped leaves and they are far less common.

Common butterwort

Scientific name: *Pinguicula vulgaris*
Height: 5–15 cm
Family: bladderwort
Flowering months: May–July

Like the sundew, common butterwort also has a flat rosette of yellowish-green leaves at its base. But unlike sundew leaves, those of the bladderwort are covered with a sticky slime. The edges of these leaves are curled inwards. Each leafless flower stem bears a single violet-coloured flower, with a two-lobed upper lip and a three-lobed lower lip. A short spur points backwards. Butterwort grows on wet rocks and in damp soil.

◀ *These yellowish-green butterwort leaves have trapped many tiny flies that cannot escape from the sticky slime.*

Common cotton grass

Scientific name: *Eriophorum angustifolium*
Height: 20–60 cm
Family: sedge
Flowering months: May–June

Despite its name, common cotton grass does not belong to the grass family. It is a spreading plant of moorland bogs, with long, narrow leaves that end in a three-sided point. The tiny flowers are clustered together in oval flower heads, which are themselves in a cluster at the top of a tall stem. Common cotton grass, and similar species such as broad-leaved cotton grass and hare's tail cotton grass are difficult to spot until the flowers are over. Then it becomes much easier, because the seed head is a highly visible mass of white cottony hairs. So in June and July, cotton grass is one of the easiest moorland plants to find.

▶ *In June and July cotton grass is easy to spot, even from quite a distance, as the white cottony seed heads dance in the breeze.*

Bog asphodel

Scientific name: *Narthecium ossifragum*
Height: 5–45 cm
Family: lily
Flowering months: July–September

When it is in flower, bog asphodel is one of the prettiest moorland wild flowers. The leaves are sword-shaped, and most of them grow in tufts at the base of the plant, but there are a few small leaves on the upright flower stem. From July to September, the bright yellow flowers can be seen. These have six 'petals', although in fact three of these are the sepals. As the flower gets older, its colour deepens to orange.

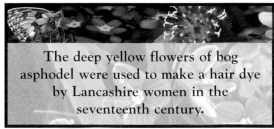

The deep yellow flowers of bog asphodel were used to make a hair dye by Lancashire women in the seventeenth century.

◀ *Bog asphodel has star-shaped flowers, each with three yellow petals and three yellow sepals.*

Be a Wild Flower Detective

Learning how to identify different species of wild flowers is a bit like detective work. Every species is different and you will need to look for clues. It is easiest to identify a wild flower when it is in bloom. Leaves provide other clues, but identifying wild flowers from their leaves alone is much more difficult. You may know the names of some wild flowers already. Look at these familiar wild flowers first, and make sure that you can recognize the sepals, petals, stamens and carpels. Then try to identify a wild flower you do not know.

WILD FLOWER DIARY

To make a wild flower diary, you will need:
- a notebook
- a camera or coloured pencils

Every month, look at the wild flowers near your home or school. Study different places, for example a garden lawn, a hedgerow, a piece of dry wasteland and a pond.

Count how many different kinds of wild flowers you can see in each different place. Identify the flowers by looking at the sepals, petals, stamens and carpels. Then look it up in this book, or other books about wild flowers.

In each entry, write down the date, the place and the different wild flowers that you can see. Take a photograph or draw a picture of each flower you see and label each picture with a caption.

Try to follow the wild flowers as they grow, flower and make their seeds. Then you will be able to draw its leaves, flowers and fruits.

Which place has the most types of wild flowers? Do some kinds of wild flowers grow in all these places, or are there different kinds of plants in each place?

▲ By keeping a wild flower diary, you can find out which flowers grow best in different places.

◄▼► White clover (left) can be identified by its cluster of small white flowers. Ragged robin (below) has ragged shaped petals. Common poppies (right) are easy to spot by their large, bright red petals.

Protecting Wild Flowers

Some wild flowers have become rare because their habitats have been changed or destroyed. The building of new houses and roads, as well as industrial development, has destroyed many wild flower habitats. Modern farming practices, such as more efficient ploughing and draining wetlands, have reduced or altered other wild flower habitats. The use of weedkillers has made many once-common farmland weeds extremely rare, and a few are now thought to be extinct in Britain.

Wild flowers can be protected in many different ways. Some farmers are now leaving strips around their fields, which are not treated with weedkillers. This means that there is a refuge for poppies, corn marigolds and other colourful farmland weeds. Many wild flowers are now protected because they are growing in nature reserves. Since no building work can take place to disrupt their habitat, the wild flowers that grow there are safe.

The law also protects wild flowers. In Britain it is illegal for anyone to dig up any wild plant without the permission of the person who owns the land. Some very rare plants are totally protected and it is an offence to pick them. This includes many kinds of orchids. It is not an offence to pick common wild flowers, but if you think you have found something rare, it is safest not to pick it.

▲ Fritillary was once widespread and abundant in wet meadows in the southern half of Britain. When many of these meadows were drained and ploughed, this plant became extremely rare.

◀ This crop is being sprayed with weedkiller, which will kill wild flowers and other farmland weeds.

Plant a Wild Flower Garden

Growing your own wild flowers is a good way to get to know many different kinds of wild flowers. You can grow wild flowers wherever you live, whether you have a garden or not. Garden centres and hardware stores sell packets of wild flower seeds.

YOU WILL NEED:

- small spade or trowel
- some packets of wild flower seeds
- a small watering can

For an indoor wild flower garden, you will also need:
- some flower pots or a small trough
- some seed compost
- old newspapers

OUTDOOR WILD FLOWER GARDEN

For an outdoor wild flower garden, first ask your parents where you can make it. Start by digging the soil using the spade or trowel until it is fine and crumbly. Remove any large stones and grass.

There are many types of wild flowers that may appear in your garden naturally. Your parents may call them weeds – especially when they grow among vegetables or in flowerbeds. Dig up some of these flowers with a small spade or trowel, and replant them in your new garden. Water them well, because moving them will have disturbed their roots and they will wilt unless they are kept moist for a few days. Now you are ready to plant some seeds.

INDOOR WILD FLOWER GARDEN

If you are making an indoor wild flower garden, spread some newspaper over a table and rest your flower pots or trough on top. Fill them with seed compost. Now you are ready to plant your seeds.

PLANTING THE SEEDS

Before you open the seed packet, read the instructions carefully. They will tell you exactly how to plant the seeds, whether they need to be lightly covered with soil or planted more deeply. Different types of seeds may need different treatments. Open the packet and plant your seeds. Water them when you first plant them and every day afterwards if the weather is hot. Seeds need water as well as warm sunshine in order to germinate and grow.

Some seedlings may appear after only a few days. Others may take one or two weeks. Many seedlings may appear very close together. When these seedlings have at least four leaves each they can be dug up gently and re-planted further apart, so that each plant has enough room to grow. Try not to damage the tiny delicate rootlets.

When your wild flowers are in bloom, watch them to see how many different kinds of insects visit the flowers. Do bees and other insects prefer the wild flowers or the garden flowers? If you have grown your wild flowers indoors, open the windows and see if any insects find your flowers. You can save some of the seeds from your flowers and plant them next year.

◀ *Packets of wild flower seeds have instructions about how to plant them. Different seeds may need to be planted differently.*

▶ *This wild flower garden contains many different flowers, including poppies, wild pansy, daisies and white campion. How many can you identify?*

Glossary

Airborne Carried along in the air.

Basal At the base, or bottom of a plant.

Bloom A flower.

Botanists People who study plants.

Bracts Leaf-like structures often found just below a flower head.

Branched Having branches.

Carpel The female organs of a flower.

Catkins Short, dangling stems bearing many tiny, usually wind-pollinated, flowers.

Compound leaf A leaf that is divided up into a number of distinct leaflets.

Corolla The petals of a flower.

Cultivated A plant that is specially grown for a particular purpose, such as decorative value, herbal or medicinal use.

Disk florets The small central florets in a flower such as a daisy.

Fertile Soil that is rich in plant nutrients.

Florets The many tiny flowerlets that make up the flower head of plants of the daisy family.

Flower heads The whole array of flowers on an individual stem.

Flower stem A stem that bears flowers.

Fruit The part of a flower that contains the seeds.

Germinate When a seed swells and starts to grow.

Glands Tiny organs that secrete, or ooze out, liquids.

Hedge banks Sloping banks with a hedge along the top.

Leaflets The leafy parts into which a compound leaf is divided.

Lobe A rounded part that hangs or sticks out.

Lobed A leaf that has a deeply wavy outline.

Nectaries Tiny organs that produce nectar, located in the base of the petals, or near the base of the petals, according to species.

Nutlets Small, hard, nutlike seeds or fruits.

Petal The usually coloured and sometimes scented part of a flower.

Photosynthesis The process that takes place in the leaves of plants that uses energy from sunlight to turn carbon dioxide in the air and water from the ground into sugar.

Ray florets The florets, each with a single narrow petal, around the outer part of a flower such as a daisy.

Ribs Veins of a leaf.

Rosette A flat circle of leaves growing out from a central root.

Runners Stems that grow horizontally over the surface of the ground.

Semi-parasite A plant or animal that gets some of its nutrients and water from the body of another plant or animal.

Sepals The parts of a flower that protect it when it is in bud.

Shrub A woody plant with many stems.

Spur A short, slender projection.

Tendrils Slender, twining structures that twist tightly around other plant stems for support.

Umbel A flower head with stems arranged like the spokes of an umbrella, with flowers at the tips of each stem.

Weed A plant that grows somewhere it is not wanted.

Whorls Rings of leaves around the stem of a plant.

Further Information

BOOKS TO READ

Collins How to Identify Wild Flowers by Christopher Grey-Wilson and Lisa Alderson (Harper Collins, 2000)

Cycles in Nature: Plant Life by Theresa Greenaway (Hodder Wayland, 2000)

Eyewitness Handbooks: Wild Flowers of Britain and Northwest Europe by Christopher Grey-Wilson (Dorling Kindersley, 1995)

New Flora of the British Isles by Clive Stace (Cambridge University Press, 1991)

Plants: British Plants, How Plants Grow by Angela Royston (Heinemann, 1999)

Straightforward Science: Plant Life by Peter Riley (Watts, 1998)

The Earth Strikes Back: Plant Life by Pamela Grant (Belitha, 1999)

The Wild Flowers of Britain and Ireland by Marjorie Blamey, Richard and Alastair Fitter (A&C Black, 2001)

Wild Flowers of the British Isles by David Streeter (Midsummer Books, 1998)

ORGANIZATIONS TO CONTACT

Most counties in Britain have their own Wildlife Trust. Each trust arranges special visits to its reserves to look at the wild flowers, and sometimes holds courses to help people identify them. Contact the address below or look on their website to find out the address of your local Wildlife Trust.

The Wildlife Trust, The Kiln, Waterside, Mather Road, Newark NG24 1WT
Tel: 01636 677711
Website: www.wildlifetrust.org.uk

Plantlife, 21 Elizabeth Street, London SW1W 9RP
Tel: 020 7808 0100
Website: www.plantlife.org.uk
This is a wild plant conservation society.

Index
Page numbers in **bold** refer to photographs.